Naming Ceremonies

Mandy Ross

Heinemann Library
Chicago, Illinois

Designed by David Poole and Geoff Ward
Originated by Dot Gradations Ltd
Printed in China by Wing King Tong

07 06 05 04 03
10 9 8 7 6 5 4 3 2 1

Library of Congress Cataloging-in-Publication Data
Ross, Mandy.
 Naming ceremonies / Mandy Ross.
 p. cm. -- (Rites of passage)
Summary: Explains the origin, historical or religious significance, and practice of naming ceremonies in different cultures around the world.
Includes bibliographical references and index.
 ISBN 1-4034-3989-3 (lib. bdg.) -- ISBN 1-4034-4597-4 (pbk.)
 1. Naming ceremonies--Juvenile literature. [1. Naming ceremonies. 2. Rites and ceremonies.] I. Title. II. Series.
 GT2435.R67 2003
 392.1′2--dc21
                    2003001899

Acknowledgments
The author and publisher are grateful to the following for permission to reproduce copyright material:
Cover photograph Panos Pictures/Jon Spaull.
p. 4 Frank Siteman/Getty Images; pp. 5, 10, 16, 23 C. Boulanger/Christine Osborne; p. 6 Penny Tweedie/Corbis; p. 7 Paul Chesley/Getty Images; p. 8 Galen Rowell/ Corbis; p. 9 John Foster/Masterfile; p. 11 Circa Photo Library; p. 12 Giacomo Pirozzi/Panos; p. 13 Roland Freeman; p. 14 Israel Talby/Israelimages.com; p. 15 Tropix; p. 17 Sandeep Mukar; p. 18 Stephen Coyne/Travel Ink; p. 19 Kristi J. Black/ Corbis; p. 20 Native Stock; p. 21 Robin Laurence/Impact; p. 22 Mohamed Ansar/Impact; p. 24 Michael S. Yamashita/Corbis; p. 25 Liba Taylor/Hutchison Library; p. 26 Origlia Franco/Corbis; p. 27 Link Picture Library; p. 28 PA; p. 29 Bojan Brecelj/Corbis.

Special thanks to both the Interfaith Education Center in Bradford, Engalnd, and Georga Godwin for their help in the preparation of this book.

Every effort has been made to contact copyright holders of any material reproduced in this book. Any omissions will be rectified in subsequent printings if notice is given to the publisher.

Some words are shown in bold, **like this.** You can find out what they mean by looking in the glossary.

Contents

What's in a Name?

Every person has a name. A name tells who a person is. A name may also tell something about a person's family, religion, and culture. When a child is born, choosing his or her name is one of the first decisions the family must make.

Many families hold a naming **ceremony** to announce the baby's name. The baby is welcomed as a new person and member of the family and culture. In this way, traditions are passed on from one **generation** to the next.

Around the world, there are many different types of naming ceremonies. In some cultures, the naming ceremony may be held at the birth itself or immediately afterward. In other cultures, naming ceremonies take place days, weeks, or months later.

This book is organized according to how soon after birth the naming ceremony happens.

By Latin American tradition, children are given both their mother's and father's surnames.

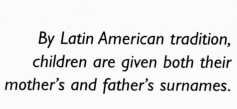

Names

Most children take the surname, or last name, of one of their parents—usually the father's. Then, the parents, sometimes with other relatives, choose one or more names to call the child. They may choose the name of a beloved relative (in some traditions a living relative, in others, someone who has died) or a religious figure. Some families consult **horoscopes** to help choose a name that will bring luck and good health.

Rites of passage

In 1909, Arnold van Gennep wrote about rites of passage. He made up the term to mean events that mark important times in a person's life. He said there are three changes in every rite of passage:
- leaving one group,
- moving on to a new stage,
- and joining a new group.

*These women are at a baby's baptism, or **Christian** naming ceremony, in Bakau, Gambia.*

5

Aboriginal Naming Ceremony

Aborigines are people whose **ancestors** lived in Australia. They lived there before people from Europe arrived in the late 18th century and took over the land. There are many different aboriginal **tribes,** each with different traditions. One tribe is the Wikmungkan people, of northeastern Australia.

Naming at birth

The Wikmungkan people carry out a naming **ritual** during the actual birth of a baby. The baby gets its birth name during this ritual. The moment after the child is born, the **midwife** shakes the **umbilical cord** and calls out the names of all of the child's living relatives, one by one. The birth name is the name that the midwife is calling when the **placenta** comes out of the mother's body. As the child grows up, he or she has a special relationship with the relative who shares that name.

This child shares its birth name with an aunt. They will have a special relationship.

Each of the Wikmungkan people also has at least two other names. Each person in a **clan** shares a name, like a surname, that relates to a particular animal. For instance, all of the men of one clan are known as Yangkaporta, which is the name of a bird. Everyone also has a personal name, like a first name, that usually relates to some feature of the clan animal.

Nomadic life

Traditionally, aboriginal people live as nomads—they move around from place to place, instead of living in a set home. However, tribes get together in great gatherings every so often during the year. Marriages and other **ceremonies** take place at these gatherings.

An aboriginal mother and grandmother carry out a ritual to protect the baby's health. Special leaves are burned, and the baby is held near the purifying smoke.

Inuit Traditions

The Inuit people live in the frozen Arctic lands of northern Canada, Alaska, and Greenland.

When an Inuit baby is a few days old, it is given its *atiq* (a-TEEK). *Atiq* means both "name" and "spirit." The *atiq* is the name of a family member who has died. It is usually a beloved older relative, such as a grandparent. The Inuit people believe that the child receives the relative's spirit, as well as his or her name.

Inuit people believe in reincarnation. They believe that after a person dies, his or her spirit starts another life within a new person. So, each new baby receives the spirit of a relative who has died. The child is both himself or herself and also the older relative. Until it receives its *atiq,* a baby is not yet thought to be a whole person.

An Inuit mother carries her child on her back.

A traditional sledge rests in front of an Inuit settlement in Nunavut, Canada.

Finding the right *atiq*

There are different ways of finding out the atiq a baby should have. If a child has a birthmark in the same place as someone who has recently died, it is a sign that they are carrying that person's spirit. Sometimes a pregnant woman dreams about a relative who has died. In the dream, the relative may ask that the new baby be named after him or her.

If a baby cries constantly, Inuit people believe it is because he or she wants to have the name or *atiq* of a dead person who has been forgotten. According to Inuit tradition, once the baby is given the right *atiq*, he or she will stop crying.

Muslim Aqiqah Ceremony

When a **Muslim** baby is born, the father or grandfather whispers a prayer in its ear. It is the first thing the child hears, and thus the child knows he or she is a Muslim.

The child must be given a name within seven days. The parents choose the name, sometimes with the help of grandparents and other relatives, too. The imam, or priest, may also suggest a name. Usually names are chosen from the Qur'an (kor-AN), the Muslim **holy** book.

A Muslim father whispers a prayer into his baby's ear.

Then, if the mother and baby are well enough, the family holds the *Aqiqah* (a-KEE-ka) **ceremony.** The Aqiqah ceremony is to thank Allah, or God, for the baby's birth and to announce the name. It is held within seven days of the birth.

At the *Aqiqah* ceremony, prayers are said to Allah while the baby's head is shaved. Then, the hair is weighed. The family gives the same weight in gold to charity, or more if they can afford it. There is also a feast for friends and relatives. Muslim boys are **circumcised,** usually within two weeks of their birth.

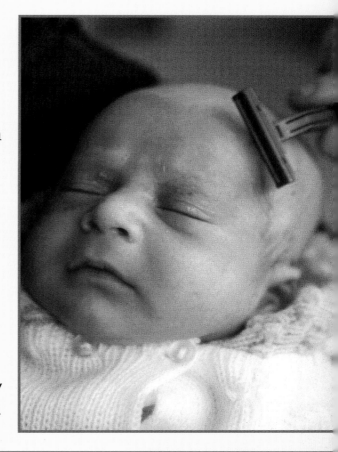

This baby's head is being carefully shaved at its Aqiqah ceremony.

Mrs. Rehman's story

Mrs. Rehman, a Muslim from Birmingham, England, has four children:

We had an Aqiqah ceremony for each of my children. Each one was a joyful time. We treat sons and daughters equally—Allah feels as much joy when a girl is born as a boy. My family helped me a lot, because I wasn't well after the births. It's very important to hold the Aqiqah ceremony, if you can. We believe that if you follow the right path from the Qur'an, then Allah will be happy and will reward you with happiness.

Yoruba Traditions

The Yoruba people live in Nigeria, in western Africa. When a Yoruba baby is born, it stays in the hut with its mother for seven days. Then, on the seventh day it is welcomed into the community with a welcome song. It feels the air, the sun, or perhaps the rain on its skin for the first time.

On the seventh day for a girl or the ninth day for a boy, a name is chosen for the baby. Yoruba children are given several names. One name tells something about how the baby was born. For instance, *Ige* means "born legs first," and *Idowu* means "child born after twins." In addition to the family name, parents may also choose a pet name, which shows their hopes for the child. For example, *Ayoke* means "one who people are happy to bless."

A Nigerian father holds his child.

Family and friends gather to welcome a baby at a Yoruba naming ceremony.

The oldest member of the family carries out the naming **ceremony,** and relatives and friends are invited. Everyone wears brightly-colored clothes, and it is a loud and lively gathering. Musicians play drums and other **percussion instruments.** Poets recite traditional poems expressing the family's hopes and prayers that the child will have a long and happy life.

At the ceremony, **symbolic** offerings are made. For instance, the baby is given a taste of honey to show the parents' prayers for a sweet life. Relatives and friends give presents of money and clothing to the family. Then, the parents announce the baby's name. Other relatives are invited to choose extra names as well. A Yoruba child may end up with twelve names, or even more.

Jewish Traditions

When a **Jewish** boy is born, he will be **circumcised** and named on the eighth day of his life, if he is healthy and strong enough. Early in the morning, relatives and friends gather either at the baby's home or at a synagogue—the Jewish place of worship. Traditionally, only boys and men are in the room when the circumcision is carried out.

After the circumcision, the baby is welcomed into the Jewish community, and his name is announced in Hebrew, the language of Jewish prayer, and their native language. Family and friends say prayers for the baby's health and wish him a happy life.

*Four **generations** of men are praying at this Jewish ceremony.*

Today, many Jewish families want to celebrate the birth of a baby girl in a similar way. The baby girl is brought to the synagogue, where she is welcomed into the Jewish community. The parents announce her name in Hebrew and in their native language, and they say a blessing. They speak of their wishes and hopes for her life.

After these **ceremonies**, relatives and friends join the family for a special meal and party to celebrate the safe arrival of the baby.

Jewish baby girls can be named any time the Torah is being read in a synagogue. A special prayer is also read for the well being of mother and daughter.

Hebrew names

Hebrew names include those of a child's parents and sometimes other relatives, too. For instance, Sam Ross's Hebrew name is Meyer ben Melech v'Rachel, which means Meyer, son of Melech and Rachel. The name " Meyer" was chosen to remember Sam's great-great-uncle Meyer, and to share an initial letter with his great-grandfather Manny, both of whom died before Sam was born.

Sikh Naming Ceremony

When a baby is born into a **Sikh** family, a naming **ceremony** is held at the *gurdwara,* the Sikh place of worship. As soon as the mother and baby are well enough, the baby is taken to the *gurdwara.* There, family and friends join in saying prayers. The parents' names are included in an important prayer called the *Ardas.*

During the naming ceremony, there is a reading from Siri Guru Granth Sahib, the Sikh **holy** scriptures. This reading is not planned, but chosen at random. The baby's parents choose a name that begins with the first letter of that reading. Every Sikh boy's name is followed by *Singh,* which means "lion." Sikh girls' names are followed by *Kaur,* or "princess."

The Siri Guru Granth Sahib is seen as a teacher among Sikhs, so the scriptures are treated with respect. At the naming ceremony, the parents give new embroidered cloths, called *rumalas,* to cover the Siri Guru Granth Sahib. It is a way of giving thanks to God for their new baby.

A Sikh family brings their baby to the gurdwara *for the naming ceremony.*

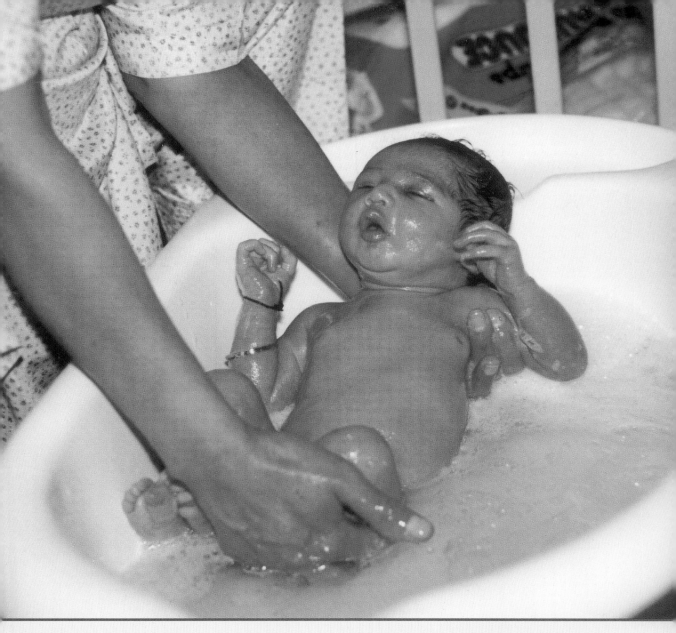

This Sikh baby is wearing his first kara, or steel bracelet—a symbol of being a Sikh.

The Five Ks

Babies are given a tiny steel bracelet, called a *kara*. It is in the shape of a circle—**symbolizing** God, who has no beginning and no end. The bracelet is one of the Five Ks worn by boys and girls. The Five Ks are the *kesh* (uncut hair), *kangha* (wooden comb), *kara* (steel bracelet), *kirpan* (symbolic sword), and *kachera* (cotton undershorts).

Buddhist Naming and Blessing

When a baby is born into a **Buddhist** family, **monks** are invited to the family's home to chant from the Buddhist **holy** writings and bless the baby.

The parents consult an **astrologer** who works out the baby's **horoscope,** based on the date, time, and place of birth. The astrologer tells the parents a lucky initial, and then the parents choose a name starting with that letter.

Most Buddhist babies will be taken to a temple, *such as this one in Sri Lanka, to be blessed.*

As soon as possible within the baby's first month of life, he or she is brought to the temple for a blessing. Parents and friends kneel and bow before a statue of Buddha, whose teachings Buddhists follow. They make offerings of flowers, candles, and **incense** to the Buddha. A monk blesses the child and announces his or her name.

A family kneels before a statue of the Buddha at a temple in Thailand.

Janaki and Aruna's story

Janaki and Aruna, Buddhists from Kandy, Sri Lanka, remember taking their baby daughter, Tharusha, to the temple:

When Tharusha was two weeks old, we took her to the main temple in Kandy to be blessed—just as we had been blessed there ourselves when we were babies. We offered Tharusha to the statue of the Lord Buddha. Then, we laid her in front of the statue while we chanted and made offerings so that she would receive blessings for a happy life. Three or four other families were blessing their babies at the same time—it was very busy and crowded, but we felt so happy!

19

Native American Baby-Naming Ceremony

The Hopis are a Native American people who live in Arizona. Hopi babies are named at a special naming **ceremony** when they are twenty days old.

Early in the morning, before dawn, a great dish of corn and lamb stew is cooked over an outdoor fire. Meanwhile, the baby is bathed and rubbed with a corn cob. For the Hopi Indians, corn is a **holy symbol** of life and well-being.

Female elders have a high position within the Hopi tribe. This Hopi gourd rattle is painted with a grandmother design.

Each guest gives a gift to the child and rubs cornmeal on the baby's forehead. Then, an older relative, usually the grandmother, takes the baby outside just as the sun is rising. The baby is held up to the rising sun, and his or her name is announced. Traditionally, the naming ceremony was held while standing on a buffalo skin. Today, there are no buffalo in the wild. Instead, the grandmother stands on a patchwork quilt. This quilt has often been stitched and given as a birth gift to the child. In this way, Native American traditions have taken on the American tradition of patchwork quilting.

Then, everyone sits on blankets on the floor indoors. A small portion of the food is put on a plate and placed on the ground just outside the door. It is a symbol of thanks to show that food comes from the earth. Everyone shares a special meal of stew, corn bread, and sweet cornmeal pudding.

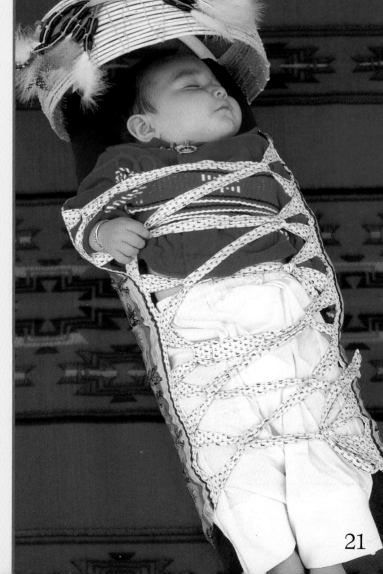

*This baby from the Navajo **tribe** is bound in the traditional style.*

Hindu Traditions

Hinduism is an ancient religion that started in India. Today, there are Hindus living in all parts of the world. Hindus pray to different forms of one god. When a baby is born in a Hindu family, the parents consult the **horoscope.** A religious teacher, called a *pundit,* tells the family the baby's lucky initial based on the date, time, and place of the baby's birth. Then, a name is chosen that starts with this letter. The baby's grandparents and other family members are often involved in choosing the name, as well as the parents:

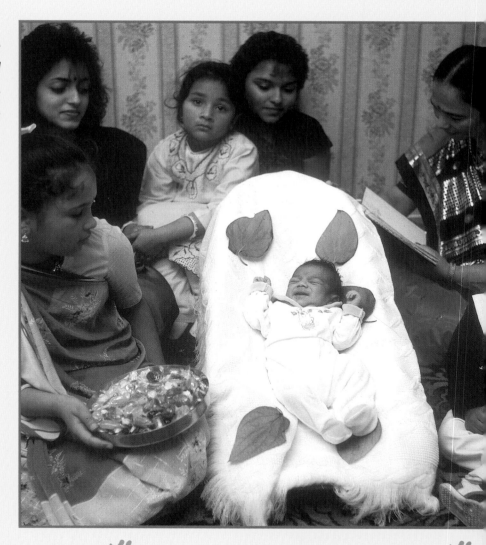

Relatives share prayers and food to celebrate the baby's safe arrival.

After 40 days, the baby is taken to the **temple,** called the *mandir.* The priest announces the baby's name and says prayers for a long life, health, and well-being. The baby is given a tiny taste of honey for a sweet life. At the temple, water is sprinkled on the baby to purify, and then sweet water, called amrit, is given for the blessings.

Later, special offerings are made to the gods when the baby eats his or her first cooked rice. This usually happens when the baby is four to six months old.

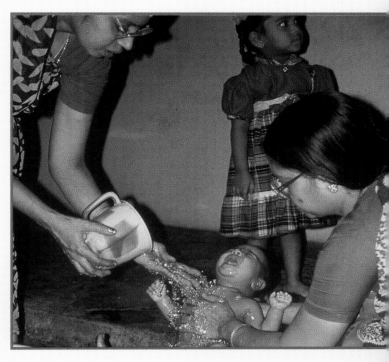

This baby is being washed as part of a Hindu religious **ceremony.**

Deepti's story

Deepti, a Hindu living in Newcastle, England, remembers when her daughter was born:

I telephoned my parents in India, and they consulted the family pundit about the baby's horoscope. The pundit gave us three lucky letters, and then we chose a name that started with one of them. My husband used the Internet to find out more about the meaning of the names we were thinking of, and the number-values of the letters. The name we chose, Karishma, has a beautiful meaning— it means " miracle."

Chinese Traditions

According to Chinese tradition, all of the children in the same **generation** share one part of their name. Brothers, sisters, and cousins all have one name that is the same, as well as their own personal name. There is a cycle of 24 generation names, so it takes hundreds of years to work through the cycle.

The baby's personal name is chosen soon after the baby is born. Rather than celebrating right away, however, the family waits 100 days. Then, they hold a Hundred Days party to celebrate the arrival of the baby. By that time, just over three months, the baby has survived the time of greatest risk. Now the family hopes that he or she can live a long and healthy life. Relatives and friends are invited to the family's home and are served tea and special foods.

Several generations of a family in Tonghai, China, posed for this picture.

At about one year old, the baby is offered a tray of objects—for instance a paint brush, small farming tools, cooking tools, and money. Whatever the baby grasps is believed to show what he or she will become as an adult. For example, a child who grasps a farming tool will become a farmer.

This baby is wearing a bonnet decorated with Chinese writing.

Chinese generation names

The Qiu family lives in London. Qiu is their family name, or **surname.** The children all share the generation name " Tai," which means "peaceful." The oldest brother is Qiu Tai Zhou. Tai Zhou means "peaceful little boat." His sister has been named Tai Shi, which means "peaceful poem." Their younger brother is called Tai Sen, which means "peaceful forest." Their cousins in southwest China share their surname and their generation name. They are called Qiu Tai Ran and Qiu Tai Shan.

Christian Traditions

Babies are named, blessed, and welcomed into the **Christian** Church usually after a few weeks or months. The traditions are slightly different in each branch of the Church. In some, there is a **ceremony** called a baptism or christening. In others, there is a service of blessing and thanksgiving for the birth of a child. In some churches, children and adults are baptized when they are older as part of a confirmation service.

On the morning of a christening or baptism, family and friends gather at the church. Often, the baby is dressed in a special white christening gown, which may have been passed down from **generation** to generation.

The Pope baptizes a baby in the Sistine Chapel at the Vatican in Italy.

The parents may have asked one or two close relatives or friends to be godparents. Godparents help the child to live as a Christian. The parents and godparents bring the child to the front of the church. They are asked to give the name they have chosen for the child, sometimes called the baby's Christian name.

The priest says prayers of blessing over water and then pours it on the baby's head and makes the sign of the cross. The water **symbolizes** washing away **sins** and making a fresh start. The priest then calls the baby by name and welcomes him or her into the Christian Church and community.

Baptism register

Each christening or baptism is recorded in the church's register of baptisms. This custom started many hundreds of years ago in Europe. The baptism register was the traditional record of births in many villages before official records began.

This baby is being baptized in a church.

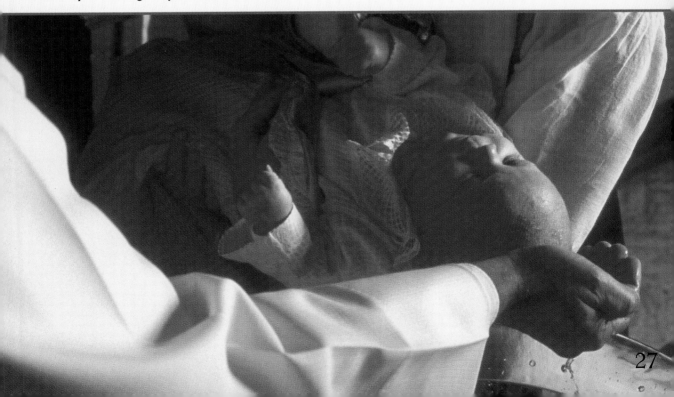

New and Old Traditions

Today, many people follow no religion. Some people want to make new, nonreligious ways of naming and celebrating their new baby. Other people look back to ancient pagan (nature-worshipping) traditions that started before **Christianity.** In some countries, **civic** officials now offer nonreligious naming **ceremonies,** just as they offer civic wedding ceremonies.

Humanists are a group of people who do not pray to a god, but who value the life of every human being. Humanists offer baby-naming ceremonies in celebration of a new life and the love between parents and their child. At a Humanist naming ceremony, friends and relatives gather to offer good wishes for the child. There may be readings of poetry and songs to celebrate the birth.

This baby was the first to be named at a civic naming ceremony in Britain.

This is a pagan ceremony in the woods in Slovenia.

Some families use an ancient pagan tradition called *saining* (SAY-ning). *Saining* was used in Europe before the beginning of Christianity. Within nine days of the child's birth, family and friends stand in a circle among woodland trees. They welcome the baby and hear its name spoken aloud, often for the first time. The child is held up to greet the earth and the sky, and then he or she is passed around the circle to be introduced to friends and family. Often, a tree is planted to **symbolize** the new life.

These new and old traditions show that, even today, people wish to celebrate the safe arrival of a new baby, just as they did in ancient times and through all of the **generations** in between.

Glossary

ancestor relative in the past. Grandparents and great-grandparents are ancestors.

astrologer someone who studies the stars and planets and the way they are supposed to affect people's lives

Buddhist person who follows the way of life taught by Buddha, who lived in ancient India about 2,500 years ago. Buddha was not a god, but a man. He taught his followers how to live simple, peaceful lives—Buddhism.

ceremony special ritual and celebration

Christian person who follows the religion of Christianity, which is based on the teachings of Jesus Christ. Christians believe that Jesus was the Son of God.

circumcise cut away the foreskin, the skin that covers the tip of the penis

civic to do with the local government; not religious

clan group of people with a common ancestor

generation all of the people born around the same time

Hindu person who follows Hinduism. Hindus worship one god (called Brahman) in many forms. Hinduism is the main religion in India.

holy special because it is to do with God or a religious purpose

horoscope prediction about a person's life, based on the position of the stars and planets when the person was born

Jew person who follows the religion of Judaism. Jews pray to one god. Their holy book is the Hebrew Bible, sometimes called the Old Testament by Christians.

midwife woman who helps in childbirth

monk member of a monastery, an all-male religious community. Monks devote their lives to God.

Muslim person who follows the religion of Islam. Muslims pray to one god, whom they call Allah.

percussion instrument musical instrument, such as drums, that are played by beating or hitting them

placenta organ by which an unborn baby is attached to the mother inside her body

ritual set of actions always done in the same way, often as a religious ceremony

Sikh person who follows the religion of Sikhism, based on the teachings of the ten Gurus, or teachers

sin action or thought that is against religious laws

surname last name

symbol picture, object, or action that stands for something else

temple building used for worship

tribe group of people who have lived together for generations

umbilical cord cord that joins a baby to its mother while it is inside her body

More Books to Read

Craven, Jerry. *Celebrations*. Vero Beach, Fla.: Rourke Publishing, 1996.

Marchant, Karena. *Hindu Festivals*. Chicago: Raintree, 2001.

Pirotta, Saviour. *Jewish Celebrations*. Chicago: Raintree, 2001.

Wallace, Paula S. *The World of Birthdays*. Milwaukee: Gareth Stevens, 2003.

Index